Why you should read this book

Both of us have had dogs of one kind or another since we were children. Although neither one of us was the primary caregivers of those dogs, we did have the responsibility of walking them. Children have entirely different expectations of their dogs than adults do. For one thing, children don't believe in leashes. And because both of us were brought up in a city, we had to train our respective dogs to stay close by during our walks. Neither one of us remembers exactly how we did that. No doubt our dogs were smarter than we were and viewed their daily outings as having to keep an eye on us rather than the other way around. Not until 1968 did we get involved in a more structured way of training. We had a landseer newfoundland and were encouraged to join the local training club. Before we knew it, a pleasant pastime turned into a hobby and then an avocation. Before long, we were conducting seminars and week-long training camps, which have taken us to almost every state in the united states, bermuda, canada, england, and puerto rico. More than 30 years later we're still sharing what we have learned along the way. Every one of our dogs has been more of a teacher than a pupil, and we have discovered much more from our dogs than we could ever have hoped to teach them. This book is our attempt to pass on to you what our dogs have taught us. Without help, few people can become proficient, much less an expert, in a given field. We certainly have had plenty of help. A well-trained dog is the result of education, more yours than your dog's. You need to know what makes a dog a dog, how he thinks, how he reacts, how he grows, how he expresses himself, what his needs are, and most important, why he does what he does. When you understand your dog fully, you can achieve a mutually rewarding relationship.

TABLE OF CONTENTS

Introduction

Most people need to know that training dogs is a fundamental concept when having dog. Simply put, the main purpose is to instill dog obedience and to establish you as the pack leader. This is also a good time to bond with the dog as training will be fun.

When can dogs be trained? Puppies have short attention spans and hence most training centre's have a minimum of 3 to 6 months for formal training. Note while dogs can still learn new tricks when they can older it gets more challenging to send them for obedience training when they are a few years old and set in their ways. You can send your dogs for training at dog training centres or you could train them yourself. Those who have prior training experience with dogs will be able to train dogs on their own.

Key Training Dog Success Factors

Consistency: use the same command and hand signal all the time. Even if the dog does not listen to the command, use the same command again instead of trying with another command

Simplicity: use simple words or signals. Only one command should be issued at one time. Don't mix commands. I was guilty of not following this when i first got involved in dog training. I used to say 'sit down' to my dog as i was thinking in english. Unfortunately, my dog does not know english and got confused if i wanted him to 'sit' or to go 'down'.

Reward: dogs love has been rewarded. Rewards should be immediate after each exercise. You can either praise or treat the dog. Note you are encouraged to say 'good boy' rather than food treats as the dog would grow to expect food treat each time it performs a command

Confident: be confident when issuing commands. Your dog would pick up your insecurities and simply would not obey.

Fun: both you and the dog should have fun. Never punish the dog if it does not do the commands properly. Instead use rewards to encourage the dogs to obey the command.

Command feasibility: it has been my experience that my german shepherd dog don't like been down in the hot ground or wet ground. Issue commands when you think the dog would also have no issue or has the ability to execute the order.

List Of Canine Good Citizen Commands

Dogs do not need to know many commands and the list below is generally sufficient. Note have a training leash handy.

- ❖ heel
- ❖ sit
- ❖ down
- ❖ come
- ❖ stand
- ❖ stay.

Dog Training: The Key To Your Dog's Safety And Your Sanity

As a gift to yourself and your dog, as well as your family and your friends and neighbors, train your dog. Doing so means sanity for you, safety for your dog, and compliments from people you meet. Make him an ambassador of goodwill for all dogs. Your dog has a life expectancy of 8 to 18 years, depending on his breed and how well you take care of him. So now is the time to ensure that these years are mutually rewarding for you and your dog.

Some dogs don't need much training, if any. They seem to just naturally fall into step with their owners' daily routines. Most, however, need at least some basic training, especially with coming when called. After all, a trained dog is a free dog. Rather than being condemned to a life on leash, he can be taken for romps in the woods and accompany his owner to many public places.

You should start training your dog the day after you bring him home, and puppies are included in this rule. Just because puppies are cute and cuddly doesn't mean they can't learn. They not only can learn, but they also learn much more quickly than an older dog. That's because they haven't acquired any bad habits.

This book gets you started on how to teach your dog to be the well-trained pet you want him to be. Believe us when we say it's well worth the investment.

What Exactly Does Training Mean?

Before you get started with training your dog, you first need to understand what training really is. The term training is used to describe two separate and distinct concepts: to teach buddy to do something that you want him to do, but that he wouldn't do on his own: for example, buddy knows how to sit and sits on his own, but you want him to sit on command, something he doesn't do on his own without training. This concept is called action training. This type of training relies mainly on using pleasant experiences, such as inducing your dog to sit with a treat. Teaching buddy the commands sit, down, stand, and come are examples of action training. to teach buddy to stop doing something he would do on his own, but that you don't want him to do: for example, buddy chases bicyclists, something he does on his own that you want him to stop doing. This concept is called abstention training. This type of training typically relies on unpleasant experiences, although it doesn't have to. In other words, the dog learns to avoid the unpleasant experience by not chasing the bicyclist or doing what you don't want him to do. For example, to teach buddy not to pull on the leash, you can use a check. A check is a crisp snap on the leash with an immediate release of tension. In order to be effective, the leash must be loose before the check is made. Buddy can avoid the check by not pulling.

 Dogs already know that avoiding unpleasant experiences is advantageous, because that's how they deal with each other. The training begins with the mother dog. When the puppies reach about 6 weeks old, she begins the weaning process. At that point in time, the puppies have sharp little teeth, which aren't very pleasant for the mother when she feeds them. She begins to growl at the puppies to communicate to them not to bite so hard. She snarls and snaps at those who ignore her growls until they stop. An offending puppy may scream to high heaven and roll over on its back, having learned its lesson. The mother dog usually follows the disagreeable experience with an agreeable one nuzzling the puppy.

HAND FEEDING

It is the foundation of a good working relationship.
Hand feeding isn't the answer to all behavioral problems, but it is a way to take a dog that has trust issues and turn them around. So whether your dog has a specific phobia or is shy around people, hand feeding is the first step to changing those behaviors. For people that are training to do competition dog sports, hand feeding is the way to get the dog to bond to you to the point that they never take their eyes off of you. For people that just want an all-around great pet, hand feeding is one of the steps i recommend. It's for any dog, any owner that wants a special bond with their dog.

In order to make training fun and enjoyable, it must be rewarding. If your dog doesn't care one way or the other about treats, doesn't like to play with toys and won't bother to walk across the room for an ear scratch, how are you going to reward him? If he sees no reason to work for what he gets because it's always available, gets it on demand, or is easily stolen, changing his meals to scheduled feedings and teaching him to work to earn can help repair a rocky relationship.

Why Hand Feed?

This is an excellent way to start off puppies.
If you do this for the first 6 months of a dog's life, you will have a dog that is more bonded to you than you have ever had before. Training will be extremely easy with those dogs. It's just getting people to actually do it. Most people say they just don't have time. But it doesn't take much more time than putting food in a bowl for the dog. This is also a great way to work your training cues while hand feeding. Remember the "nothing in life is free" rule! It's easy to have a well mannered dog; you just need to put the time and commitment into him or her!
Hand feeding teaching the dog to focus on you! You control the food, the goodies, and the treats. And you are making them work for it, even better yet! This makes for a non demanding dog, or a request barker later.

If your dog is pushy, bossy, or rude, hard to motivate, disinterested, or has its own agenda, (or even if it isn't) hand feeding will improve your relationship with your dog.

Teachings your dog to have manners around food

ability to drop everything and come when called

slow down fast eaters...

So How Do You Do This?

Find a spot on the floor, this can be where your pup or dog eats now, or better yet, for socialization, you can feed him in different areas of the house. Put the dog food in his bowl. Hand out the kibble here and there without asking the dog to do anything. If the dog naturally comes to you, immediately give the dog some of it's kibble. If they are sitting there staring at you, give them a few pieces. Make sure not to reward bad behavior. If you give a dog kibble that is jumping up, barking, pawing at you, or misbehaving, then you reward that bad behavior, you don't want that. So i ask that the dog is standing or sitting patiently, acting calm before you hand feed them. Once the dog has the routine down, start asking the dog to do things for the food. Sit, watch me, down, shake, spin, and so on. Great time to work in your training skills you learned in class. So in the end, they are working for every kibble they eat. "nothing in life is free" rule. Dogs want a leader, and they want a job. By doing this, you accomplish both.

It doesn't have to be just one person in the house that is feeding the dog as long as the food is pre measured so you don't over or under feed the dog. Kids do really well with this. And you wouldn't believe the bonding and understanding that kids and dogs have when they have hand fed. This will also help with the recall. A dog that is hand fed will almost always come to your hand if you put it out. You just better not try to trick them too many times by not having food in it or they get wise to this trick have you ever seen the dogs that never take their eyes off their owners? Hand feeding is the way to accomplish that.

 yes, hand feeding can be a pain. And yes, you have to be committed to doing it for months to make it work.

HOW TO CRATE TRAIN YOUR DOG

Crate training your dog may take some time and effort, but can be useful in a variety of situations. If you have a new dog or puppy, you can use the crate to limit his access to the house until he learns all the house rules - like what he can and can't chew on and where he can and can't eliminate.

A crate is also a safe way of transporting your dog in the car, as well as a way of taking him places where he may not be welcome to run freely. If you properly train your dog to use the crate, he'll think of it as his safe place and will be happy to spend time there when needed.

Selecting a crate

Crates will be plastic, (often called flight kennels or vary-kennels) or collapsible, metal pens. They come in different sizes and can be purchased at most pet supply stores. Your dog's crate should be just large enough for him to stand up and turn around.

The crate training process

Crate training can take days or weeks, depending on your dog's age, temperament and past experiences. It's important to keep two things in mind while crate training. The crate should always be associated with something pleasant, and training should take place in a series of small steps - don't go too fast.

Step 1: Introducing Your Dog To The Crate

Put the crate in an area of your house where the family spends a lot of time, such as the family room. Put a soft blanket or towel in the crate. Bring your dog over to the crate and talk to him in a happy tone of voice. Make sure the crate door is securely fastened open, so it won't hit your dog and frighten him.

To encourage your dog to enter the crate, drop some small food treats near it, then just inside the door, and finally, all the way inside the crate. If he refuses to go all the way in at first, that's okay - don't force him to enter. Continue tossing treats into the crate until your dog will walk calmly all the way into the crate to get the food. If he isn't interested in treats, try tossing a favorite toy in the crate. This step may take a few minutes or as long as several days.

Step 2: Feeding Your Dog His Meals In The Crate

After introducing your dog to the crate, begin feeding him his regular meals near the crate. This will create a pleasant association with the crate. If your dog is readily entering the crate when you begin step 2, put the food dish all the way at the back of the crate. If your dog is still reluctant to enter the crate, put the dish only as far inside as he will readily go without becoming fearful or anxious. Each time you feed him, place the dish a little further back in the crate.

Once your dog is standing comfortably in the crate to eat his meal, you can close the door while he's eating. At first, open the door as soon as he finishes his meal. With each successive feeding, leave the door closed a few minutes longer, until he's staying in the crate for 10 minutes or so after eating. If he begins to whine to be let out, you may have increased the length of time too quickly. Next time, try leaving him in the crate for a shorter time period. If he does whine or cry in the crate, it's imperative that you not let him out until he stops. Otherwise, he'll learn that the way to get out of the crate is to whine, so he'll keep doing it.

Step 3: Conditioning Your Dog To The Crate For Longer Time Periods

After your dog is eating his regular meals in the crate with no sign of fear or anxiety; you can confine him there for short time periods while you're home. Call him over to the crate and give him a treat. Give him a command to enter such as, "kennel up." encourage him by pointing to the inside of the crate with a treat in your hand. After your dog enters the crate, praise him, give him the treat and close the door.

Sit quietly near the crate for five to 10 minutes and then go into another room for a few minutes. Return, sit quietly again for a short time, then let him out of the crate. Repeat this process several times a day. With each repetition, gradually increase the length of time you leave him in the crate and the length of time you're out of his sight. Once your dog will stay quietly in the crate for about 30 minutes with you out of sight the majority of the time, you can begin leaving him crated when you're gone for short time periods and/or letting him sleep there at night. This may take several days or several weeks.

Step 4 Part A: Crating Your Dog When Left Alone

After your dog is spending about 30 minutes in the crate without becoming anxious or afraid, you can begin leaving him crated for short periods when you leave the house. Put him in the crate using your regular command and a treat. You might also want to leave him with a few safe toys in the crate. You'll want to vary at what point in your "getting ready to leave" routine you put your dog in the crate. Although he shouldn't be crated for a long time before you leave, you can crate him anywhere from five to 20 minutes prior to leaving. Don't make your departures emotional and prolonged, but matter-of-fact. Praise your dog briefly, give him a treat for entering the crate and then leave quietly.

When you return home, don't reward your dog for excited behavior by responding to him in an excited, enthusiastic way. Keep arrivals low key. Continue to crate your dog for short periods from time to time when you're home so he doesn't associate crating with being left alone. Your dog should not be left alone in the crate for more than four to five hours at a time during the day.

Part b: crating your dog at night

Put your dog in the crate using your regular command and a treat. Initially, it may be a good idea to put the crate in your bedroom or nearby in a hallway, especially if you have a puppy. Puppies often need to go outside to eliminate during the night, and you'll want to be able to hear your puppy when he whines to be let outside. Older dogs, too, should initially be kept nearby so that crating doesn't become associated with social isolation. Once your dog is sleeping comfortably through the night with his crate near you, you can begin to gradually move it to the location you prefer.

Potential Problems

Too Much Time In The Crate:

A crate isn't a magical solution. If not used correctly, a dog can feel trapped and frustrated. For example, if your dog is crated all day while you're at work and then crated again all night, he's spending too much time in too small a space. Other arrangements should be made to accommodate his physical and emotional needs. Also remember that puppies under six months of age shouldn't stay in a crate for more than three or four hours at a time. They can't control their bladders and bowels for longer periods.

Whining:

If your dog whines or cries while in the crate at night, it may be difficult to decide whether he's whining to be let out of the crate, or whether he needs to be let outside to eliminate. If you followed the training procedures outlined above, your dog hasn't been rewarded for whining in the past by being released from his crate. Try to ignore the whining. If your dog is just testing you, he'll probably stop whining soon. Yelling at him or pounding on the crate will only make things worse.

If the whining continues after you've ignored him for several minutes, use the phrase he associates with going outside to eliminate. If he responds and becomes excited, take him outside. This should be a trip with a purpose, not play time. If you're convinced that your dog doesn't need to eliminate, the best response is to ignore him until he stops whining. Don't give in, otherwise you'll teach your dog to whine loudly to get what he wants.

If you've progressed gradually through the training steps and haven't done too much too fast, you'll be less likely to encounter this problem. If the problem becomes unmanageable, you may need to start the crate training process over again.

Separation Anxiety

Attempting to use the crate as a remedy for separation anxiety won't solve the problem. A crate may prevent your dog from being destructive, but he may injure himself in an attempt to escape from the crate. Separation anxiety problems can only be resolved with counterconditioning and desensitization procedures.

POTTY TRAINING YOUR DOG

Decide on a "potty training command" for your puppy We suggest the plain and simple: "let's go make!". Be sure that everyone in your household uses the same command with your dog, as consistency is vital.

Getting started

We feel the best time to start potty training your puppy is first thing in the morning when you know your dog really has to make! While stating your "potty training command", take your dog's paw and gently swat it against the dog training bells. Since he will be needing to make urgently, only guide them to ring the bells a couple of quick times. While doing this, give them words of encouragement such as: "good boy, good bells" and "ring the bells, let's go make!". Note: if your dog is so tiny that they can't reach the bells while standing, gently pop your dog up onto their back legs and guide a front paw to the bells.

Do not give them treats at this time. You don't want to accidentally train your dog to think that ringing the bell is a trick! Only after your dog goes out to make (and actually makes!) Do you then reward them with a treat. Again, no treat unless they actually relieve themselves!

Repetition

Repeat the above training method every time you take them out to make. Be consistent and diligent with this training, and your dog will soon be ringing the bells by themselves!
It's also critical that you continue to praise your puppy when they ring the dog training bells, as it will further reinforce this positive style of communicating their needs.

Additionally, if you have several dogs in your household, they can all be bell trained simultaneously. It doesn't matter if you are potty training a puppy or an old dog, they can all learn to use bells! Some dogs catch on in days, while others take longer - even up to 4 weeks. Be patient and, again, use lots of positive reinforcement. Once your dog has mastered the bell ringing, feel free to take your dog training bells on the road to grandma's house - or even a hotel room! Immediately show your dog where you've hung their bells. Then they will know, wherever the bells are hanging, is the door they will use to go outside to make.

By following these simple rules, you should soon be well on the way to successfully potty training your dog.

A POTENTIAL LIFE SAVER "COME"

Why teach your dog to come to you? This is the ultimate in safety cues! If your dog ever escapes the home you will want to have a solid foundation for this behavior to potentially save his life. It is also a great way to direct him onto something else. If he is about to check out what's in the trash, call "come!" (and give him his reward as you cover the trash can.)

Teaching The Basic Behavior, "Come"

❖ Find a quiet place to practice and get your clicker, treats and dog. Put a treat on the floor for your dog to eat and walk to the other side of the room. Hold your hand out with a treat visible and say your dog's name if he is not looking at you. Once you get his attention (or if you already have it), say "come" in a normal/happy tone of voice. Click when your dog begins to come to you. Praise him the rest of the way and give him a treat when he gets to you. While you reward him, touch his collar (this is a good idea in case your dog ever decides to play the grab the treat and run game!). Practice this about 10 times and take a break. Alternatively you can play this with a second person and "ping pong" him back and forth.

❖ Begin the exercise in the same way as above, hold your hand out as if you have a treat in it, but it will be empty (we will fool him a bit!). Click him for beginning to come and treat him when he gets to you from your pouch or pocket. Repeat 10 times and take a break.
❖ Continue practicing using the empty-hand. This is now a "hand signal"! If you would like, you can also fade this so that the dog responds to the verbal cue alone.

Becoming An Expert At Coming

❖ Practice out of sight, outside and in more distracting environments as detailed on the worksheet.

❖ **Decoy exercise:** one person is the "handler" and will call the dog. The other person is a "teaser" and will try to tempt the dog with food or a toy. If the dog goes toward them while the handler is calling, the teaser should ignore the dog and turn away. When the dog finally comes to the handler, he gets rewards from both the handler and the teaser.

❖ **Fetch-interrupt exercise:** toss a ball or piece of food. As the dog is chasing it call him. If he comes after getting the ball/treat he gets clicked and one small treat. If he comes before getting the ball/food he gets a click and jackpot. Sometimes you might need a little luring to get him started: toss the ball/food and then quickly put your treat to his nose, click and jackpot if he comes directly to you then fade the lure out.

Alternatively if your dog will fall for it you can try faking him out by making the appropriate motions but not throwing anything. This is a great game to play with his meal of dry food – toss one piece of food, if he interrupts chasing it to come to you when you call, click and give him a whole handful of it.

- ❖ **Hide and seek:** when you are outside together and your dog is wandering around and seems to have forgotten you exist, hide behind a tree. When your dog comes looking for you c/t and make a big deal of him. Always work in a safe area.

Tips:

- ❖ Never call your dog for something he may feel is unpleasant. For example when leaving the park, call your dog, put his leash on and play for a bit longer before exiting.

- ❖ Make coming to you always fabulous! Always treat, use the jackpot, and occasionally bring out a ball from your pocket and throw it or play a little chase as an additional reward.

- ❖ If your dog does not respond when you call and you must get him, try these tricks: running backwards away from the dog, crouching down, clapping your hands, whistling, squeaking a toy, or showing him food. Do not run towards him as this is an invitation to play "catch me" and humans usually lose this game! Once he comes to you he must always be rewarded, even if he didn't come initially and stressed you out in the process!

- ❖ C/t your dog for "checking in" when you haven't cued it and he's off lead.

- ❖ Practice "come" at least 5 times per day (forever!).

- ❖ Work in a fenced area or use a "long line"- get a light clothesline rope and knot it every couple of feet. Let your dog drag this and practice in a park or field. Make sure it is long enough so that you will be able to step on it if he decides to "take off". It is safest for your dog to attach the rope to a body harness instead of a neck collar.

❖ Have two "come" cues, one that means a great food treat is not necessarily involved (as in "cum'ere and sit on the sofa with me") and another that means "i have great stuff!"

A POTENTIAL LIFE SAVER "DROP IT"

Why teach a dog to "drop it"? If you have a young puppy, you know the answer to this - it's because they frequently have something valuable or dangerous in their mouths! The goal is that when you cue "drop it", your dog will open her mouth releasing whatever was in there and allow you to retrieve the item. It is very important to make sure your dog is making a good bargain with you for her prize (you give her a good treat) and that you stay calm and don't chase her. If this is taught correctly, your dog will be happy to hear you say "drop it". If your dog isn't happy to hear "drop it" for all items yet, then it is best keep those items out of reach until you have practiced with them. This exercise is also important because it can prevent food guarding. If your dog knows that you do not "steal" she will not worry about you approaching favorite items.

Teaching "drop it":

* Get together a few items your dog might like to chew on, your clicker and some good treats like cheese or turkey. (i'm sure you now have your dog's attention!)
* Have a piece of food ready in your other hand as you encourage your dog to chew on one of the objects. Once she has her mouth on it, put a piece of food close to her nose and say "drop it". Click when she opens her mouth and feed her the treat as you pick up the item with your other hand. Return the item to her.

* Try to get her to pick up the object again so you can continue practicing, but beware that once your dog knows there are treats involved she may want to keep her mouth free for eating! In this case, keep your

Treats handy throughout the day and whenever you see her randomly pick up an object or toy you can practice. Aim for at least 10 repetitions per day. Occasionally you will not be able to give her the object back (if she's found a forbidden object), but that's okay just be sure to give her an extra nice treat.

* Once you've completed about 10 repetitions, repeat the process in #2 exactly, but this time you will be sneaky and won't actually have the treat in the hand that you put close to her nose (i call this "empty fingers"). She will most likely drop the object anyway and you can click and get the treat out of your pouch. Give her the equivalent of 3 treats the first time you use empty fingers and she drops the item.

* After a few days of practicing, try it with a tasty item. Get a carrot or hard chew. Hold it in your hand and offer the other side of the

item to your dog to chew on – but don't let go! Let her put her mouth on it and then cue "drop it". Give her the equivalent of 3 treats the first time she does this and offer her the object again. If your dog won't retake the item, just put it away and practice another time. Get 10 reps of this before going forward.

❖ Now get your hard chew again and some really fresh yummy treats (meat or cheese). This time you will offer the object to your dog and let go and then right away cue "drop it". When she does give her the equivalent of your extra yummy treats and then give her the item to keep (this should make a very good impression!). If she doesn't release the item, try showing her your treat first and if that doesn't work, just let her have it and try again later with a lower value food-related item. You will be able to build up to the highest value items once your dog realizes it is worth her while to listen.

❖ Practice the "drop it" with real-life objects around that she enjoys but are not allowed such as: tissues, pens (begin with an empty one), wrappers, shoes, etc. Then practice this outside!

Tips:

❖ If your dog already enjoys grabbing objects and having a game of chase, you should begin by teaching her that you will not chase her. Just ignore her and then she will probably drop the item on her own once she is bored of it. You can also try distracting her by ringing the doorbell or knocking on the door.

❖ If your dog will not drop a dangerous item, even for a yummy treat (or if you don't have one at the moment shame on you!) Place your fingers on the lips of her upper jaw where her canines are and push in and pull up. This will open her mouth so you can retrieve the item. Make sure you give her a big reward (even if you're frustrated) for allowing this invasive treatment and keep that item out of reach in the future until you are ready to teach her to drop it.

❖ It's okay to show her a treat (bribe her) if she has a forbidden item that is higher in value than what she has been training with. Be careful not to make a habit of this!

❖ Practice "drop it" during tug and fetch games.

POTENTIAL LIFE SAVER"LEAVE IT"

Why teach your dog to "leave it"? The goal is to have your dog take his attention away from an object of interest when you cue "leave it". This is important when the item of interest is unsafe, such dropped medication and is also a useful self-control exercise.

❖ Have treats hidden in both of your fists. Let him sniff one of your fists. Click and treat (c/t) when he eventually looks away from your fist and feed the treat with your other hand. Repeat until he no longer tries to get the treat from your fist when you present it.

- ❖ Open your hand containing the treat and show him the treat. Close it if he tries to get the treat. Repeat until he decides to ignore the treat while your hand is open and then c/t by feeding a treat with your other hand. Repeat the exercise until every time you present your open "decoy" hand with a treat in it he ignores it right away. At this point, add the cue "leave it" (say this just once for each repetition of the exercise) as you show him the decoy treat. Repeat.
- ❖ Set the treat on the floor and say "leave it". Cover the treat with your hand if he tries to get it. C/t when he looks away from the treat. Repeat the exercise until he doesn't try to get the treat from the floor once you say **"leave it"**. Repeat.

- ❖ Set the treat on the floor, say "leave it" and stand up. Cover it with your foot if he tries for it. C/t for ignoring the treat. Repeat.

- ❖ Walk him past the treat on leash, say "leave it" when he sees the treat and keep him from getting it with the leash. C/t when he ignores the decoy treat on the floor. Repeat

- ❖ Next have fun and increase the length of time that he leaves it or stack treats on his paws or toss them around.

- ❖ Teach him that "leave it" also applies to objects such as toys and living things. By beginning with something very easy and building up to the more difficult.

A POTENTIAL LIFE SAVER "SIT"

Why Teach Your Dog To Sit?

He will learn that in order to get good-stuff-for-dogs he had better put his fanny on the ground and this is a good default behavior. It is very simple to teach; it helps establish human leadership and is a great substitute for jumping up and lots of other problems.

Teaching The Basic Behavior, Sit:

- ❖ Find a quiet place to practice and get your clicker, treats and dog. Wait for him to sit. When his bum hits the floor click and treats (c/t). Feed the treat while he is sitting and then toss another treat to get him up again. Continue to practice until your dog is sitting again right away after you feed his treat.

- ❖ Now say "sit" just as he begins to do so and c/t. From now on you will only reward sits that you have cued.

Becoming An Expert At Sitting:

- ❖ Practice for 5 minutes, twice per day by asking him to "sit" in increasingly distracting situations. Use the chart provided to track your progress.

- ❖ Practice "go crazy and sit": run around with your dog while squeaking a toy and then ask him to sit. C/t success.

❖ "say please": ask your dog to sit whenever you give him something he likes such as access to outside, his food bowl, or petting.

❖ If you are having trouble, don't get frustrated, just back up a step, succeed at that, take a break and then try again later (maybe with better treats).

Please read this section extremely carefully. I shall repeat over and over: teaching bite inhibition is the most important aspect of your puppy's entire education.

Certainly puppy biting behavior must eventually be eliminated. We cannot have an adult dog playfully mauling family, friends, and strangers in the manner of a young puppy. However, it is essential that this be done gradually and progressively via a systematic two-step process: first, to inhibit the force of puppy bites and second, to lessen the frequency of puppy mouthing.

Ideally, the two phases should be taught in sequence, but with more active puppy biters you may wish to work on both stages at the same time. In either case, you must teach your puppy to bite or mouth gently before puppy biting behavior is eliminated altogether.

INHIBITING THE FORCE OF BITES.

The first step is to stop your puppy from hurting people: to teach him to inhibit the force of his play-bites. Physical punishments are certainly not called for. But it is essential to let your puppy know that bites can hurt. A simple "ouch!" is usually sufficient. When the puppy backs off, take a short time-out to "lick your wounds," instruct your pup to come, sit, and lie down to apologize and make up and then, resume playing. If your puppy does not respond to your yelp by easing up or backing off, an effective technique is to call the puppy a "bully!" and then leave the room and shut the door. Allow the pup a minute or two time-out to reflect on the association between his painful bite and the immediate departure of his favorite human playmate. Then return to make up. It is important to show that you still love your puppy, only that his painful bites are objectionable. Have your pup come and sit and then resume playing once more.

It is much better for you to walk away from the pup than to physically restrain him or remove him to his confinement area at a time when he is biting too hard. So make a habit of playing with your puppy in his long-term confinement area. This technique is remarkably effective with lead-headed dogs, since it is precisely the way puppies learn to inhibit the force of their bites when playing with each other. If one puppy bites another too hard, the bite yelps and playing is postponed while he licks his wounds. The biter soon learns that hard bites interrupt an otherwise enjoyable play session. He learns to bite more softly once play resumes.

The next step is to eliminate bite pressure entirely, even though the "bites" no longer hurt. While your puppy is chewing his human chew toy, wait for a bite that is harder than the rest and respond as if it really hurt, even though it didn't: "ouch, you worm! Gauntly! That really hurt me, you bully!" your puppy begins to think, "good heavens! These humans are soooooo sensitive. I'll have to be really careful when mouthing their delicate skin." and that's precisely what you want your pup to think: that he needs to be extremely careful and gentle when playing with people.

Your pup should learn not to hurt people well before he is three months old. Ideally, by the time he is four-and-a-half months old before he develops strong jaws and adult canine teeth he should no longer be exerting any pressure when mouthing.

Decreasing The Frequency Of Mouthing

Once your puppy has been taught to mouth gently, it is time to reduce the frequency of mouthing. Your pup must learn that mouthing is okay, but he must stop when requested. Why? Because it is inconvenient to drink a cup of tea or to answer the telephone with fifty pounds of wriggling pup dangling from your wrist. That's why.

It is better to first teach "off" using food as both a distraction and a reward. The deal is this: once i say "off," if you don't touch the food treat in my hand for just one second, i'll say, "take it" and you can have it. Once your pup has mastered this simple task, up the ante to two or three seconds of non-contact, and then to five, eight, twelve, twenty, and so on. Count out the seconds and praise the dog with each second: "good dog one, good dog two, good dog three," and so forth. If the pup touches the treat before you are ready to give it, simply start the count from zero again. Your pup quickly learns that once you say "off," he cannot have the treat until he has not touched it, for, say, eight seconds, so the quickest way to get the treat is not to touch it for the first eight seconds. In addition, regular hand-feeding during this exercise encourages your pup's soft mouth.

Once your pup understands the "off" request, use food as a lure and a reward to teach it to let go when mouthing. Say, "off" and waggle some food as a lure to entice your pup to let go and sit. Then praise the pup and give the food as a reward when he does so.

The main point of this exercise is to practice stopping the pup from mouthing, and so each time your puppy obediently ceases and desists, resume playing once more. Stop and start the session many times over. Also, since the puppy wants to mouth, the best reward for stopping mouthing is to allow him to mouth again. When you decide to stop the mouthing session altogether, say, "off" and then offer your puppy a kong stuffed with kibble. If ever your pup refuses to release your hand when requested, say, "bully!" rapidly extricate your hand from his mouth, and storm out of the room mumbling, "right. That's done it! You've ruined it! Finished! Over! No more!" and shut the door in his face. Give the pup a couple of minutes on his own to reflect on his loss and then go back to call him to come and sit and make up before continuing the mouthing game.

By the time your pup is five months old, he must have a mouth as soft and reliable as a fourteen-year-old working labrador retriever: your puppy should never initiate mouthing unless requested; he should never exert any pressure when mouthing; and he should stop mouthing and calm down immediately upon request by any family member. Whether or not you allow your adult dog to mouth on request is up to you. For most owners, i recommend that they teach their dog to discontinue mouthing people altogether by the time he is six to eight months old. However, it is essential to continue bite inhibition exercises. Otherwise, your dog's bite will begin to drift and become harder as he grows older. It is important to regularly hand feed your dog and clean his teeth each day, since these exercises involve a human hand in his mouth.

For owners who have good control over their dog, there is no better way to maintain the dog's soft mouth than by regular play-fighting. However, to prevent your puppy from getting out of control and to fully realize the many benefits of play-fighting, you must play by the rules and teach your dog to play by the rules.

Play-fighting teaches your puppy to mouth only hands, which are extremely sensitive to pressure, but never clothing. Shoelaces, ties, trousers, and hair have no nerves and cannot feel. Therefore you cannot provide the necessary feedback when your pup begins to mouth too hard and too close to your skin. The play-fighting game also teaches your dog that he must adhere to rules regarding his jaws, regardless of how worked up he may be. Basically, play-fighting gives you the opportunity to practice controlling your puppy when he is excited. It is important to establish such control in a structured setting before real-life situations occur.

TEACHING YOUR DOG TO LOVE THE WATER

Dogs are natural swimmers, right? Actually, no they aren't! Dogs instinctively tread water if they fall in it's called dog paddling but that isn't the same as knowing how to swim. That's why all dogs need to be properly introduced to water. The first, most crucial step is obedience training, because a dog who disobeys you on land will definitely defy you in the pool, lake or ocean. After that, follow this advice to keep your pet healthy and happy.

Here are some pointers for making sure your dog can make a graceful and lifesaving exit.

First, carry the dog into the pool, set him gently into the water, and help him swim to the steps. Then reward and repeat several times until he gets the idea. When he makes it to the steps easily, move to next exercise. Make sure to offer abundant rewards—praise or toys. You want the dog to view reaching the steps as a great cause for celebration.

Turn away from the steps and bring the dog into the pool and guide him lightly around and to the steps. After one or two times most dogs will aim for the steps naturally. Some water-loving breeds may not want to get out, but all dogs need to know how to exit. So be persistent in getting them to reach the goal before you let them free to swim joyously!

Teach the dog to reach the step from anywhere in the pool by putting him in the water at different points and guiding him to the exit. This is something dogs pick up quickly. The steps are the reward now! Knowing where the steps are eliminates a panic if the dog falls or is knocked into the pool while playing.

Other Water Health Tips

* Don't let your dog drink swimming water. Lakes and rivers can host parasites and algae, pool water are chlorinated, and ocean water is salty; none of these are good for your dog. Keep a dish of

fresh water available for your pet.

* ❖ Rinse off dogs after swimming to get rid of chlorine and salt water, which can dry their skin. Dry their ears afterward, too, to help prevent infection.

* ❖ Of course, you should always supervise your dogs around water, but by following these easy exercises, you can make sure that your pool parties will be occasions for a lot of wagging, wet tails.

CORRECTING TYPICAL BEHAVIORAL PROBLEM FOR YOUR PUPPY

Leash Manners:

Imagine your dog walking happily by your side, stopping when you stop, turning when you turn and continuing with you past other dogs and people. He doesn't pull on the leash and he only goes potty and sniffs when you give permission. It is the most challenging thing you will probably teach him to do, but it is fun too! Read on to begin make this vision a reality. A head collar (such as a gentle leader or halti) or front-attachment harness (such as an easy walk) can help to discourage your dog from pulling, but he will need training to learn to walk beside you without pulling at all.

A front-attachment harness is a safe and easy to use no-pull device that is great for all dogs. Choose a head collar for dogs with aggressive tendencies or for those that need the maximum amount of control such as a small owner with giant-breed dog. The front-attachment harness and head collar should only be used with leashes that are a maximum of

6 feet long. If the leash is too long, it is possible that he could get going fast enough to hurt himself if he were to hit the end of the leash abruptly. A simple way to help your dog learn to walk without pulling on the leash is to stop moving forward when he pulls and to reward him with treats when he walks by your side.

If your dog is not very interested in food treats, then you can a tug a toy or toss a ball for him whenever feeding a treat or giving a reward is mentioned. The steps below will go into more detail in order to help you to teach him how to have excellent leash manners.

Step 1: "Walking With My Person Is Delicious!"

Start by attaching your dog to a rope, or leash that is 10-20 feet long (but not retractable), while he is wearing a standard harness. Get some pea-sized pieces of fresh meat or cheese to use to reward your dog and go to a familiar outdoor area like your backyard.
Decide whether you prefer your dog to walk on your left or right. Whichever side you choose (left is traditional), you will feed him his treat reward right by your thigh on that side. He will soon begin to seek out that side since that is where yummy treats come from! Walk briskly and randomly around your yard. Whenever your dog happens to choose to walk beside you, reward him click and feed your treat next to your thigh on your preferred side. If he continues walking next to you, c/t every step you take together. Don't worry, as he gets better at this you will not need to reward him as often. Practice until your dog is staying beside you more often than not as you walk

Step 2: "It's Worth My While To Watch Where My Person Is Going And Go Along Too!"

Begin walking about your yard. Wait for a moment when your dog is walking off on his own, or is lagging behind to sniff or go potty. Say "let's go" in an upbeat voice, slap your thigh the first few times to make sure that he notices you and turn and walk away from your dog.

If he catches up with you before the leash gets tight c/t by feeding a few treats to him next to your preferred side and then c/t every couple of steps if he continues to stay with you as you walk.

If he catches up to you after the leash gets tight do not give him a reward but instead say "let's go" again

While you still have his attention and c/t after he takes a couple of steps with you. C/t for every couple of steps you take together if he chooses to continue walking by your side. If he does not come towards you after you've said "let's go" and the leash has gotten tight, stop walking while continuing to apply gentle leash pressure. Praise him and release the pressure once he begins to come towards you. When he gets to you, do not give him a reward but instead say "let's go" again while you still have his attention. C/t after he takes a couple of steps with you and for every couple of steps, if he continues to stay with you as you walk.

Continue to practice this step until he is staying by your side most of the time while you walk in your backyard and if he veers off away from your side, saying "let's go", gets him coming back to you.

Step 3: "I Know When It's Time To Smell (Or To Pee On) The Roses"

Your dog needs time sniff and to go potty while on the leash, but it will help him to learn better manners if you decide when that will be. As you are practicing your leash walking with your dog, about every 5 minutes, at a time when you would usually c/t, instead say something like "go sniff" and let him sniff around or go potty while he is on the leash. This is a privilege or reward, so if he pulls on the leash during this free time say "lets go" and walk in the opposite direction, thereby ending the free time. When you are ready to end the free-time, say "let's go" and begin walking.

Step 4: "Sometimes I Really Need To Pay Attention To Where My Person Is Going!"

Continue practicing leash walking in your yard as in steps 1 through 3 but by using a shorter leash. Eventually reduce the leash length to 6 feet. Practice walking extra fast or slow, stopping or changing directions. C/t if he/she is able stay by your side during these challenges.

Begin to c/t him/her less frequently for walking by your side but be sure to continue to c/t him when it was challenging for him/her because you changed directions or there was a distraction.

Taking It To The Street:

On your neighborhood walks you will apply the same techniques as you did in your yard, but now there will be additional distractions and challenges such as friendly strangers, squirrels and other dogs. Consider using a front-attachment harness or head collar for extra control and bringing fresh meat or cheese for use as treats.

Say "let's go" and walk in the opposite direction when he forgets about you or pulls, and reward him with treats when he walks beside you. Be sure to reward him with extra treats when it was extra difficult for him to pay attention to you. Don't forget sniff breaks!

Red Light Green Light Exercise:

Outfit your dog in a standard harness attached to a 6 foot leash. Hold your dog's leash and toss a ball or treat 20 feet away from you and your leashed dog. If he pulls toward the object, say "let's go" and turn and walk in the opposite direction. If he walks beside you while you walk towards it allow him to continue towards the object until he reaches it and can take it as his reward. Use a longer leash or a less desirable object if you need to make this easier for him at first.

Leash Manners Troubleshooting:

If your dog is crossing in front of you stomp or shuffle your feet a bit to make your presence known. If he is lagging behind a great deal, he may probably be frightened or not feeling well, so use lots of encouragement instead of pulling him along. If he is lagging to sniff or to potty, simply keep walking but be sure to apply only gentle pressure on the leash. Don't forget to use lots of rewards when he does walk with you.

Heel:

Teaching him to heel is useful for short periods when you need him very close to you and paying attention. It can be very helpful when walking him past distractions like other animals.
Begin practicing in your home. Place a treat in your fist and let him sniff it. Say "heel" and take a couple of steps leading him along with the treat in your fist near your thigh. C/t when he is following your fist with his nose.
Now, practices having your dog follow your empty fist. C/t for every couple of steps that he follows the fist. Continue practicing "heel" and increasing your standards each session. Your closed fist will remain as a "hand signal" for heel.

Try this outside and in more distracting circumstances.

STOPPING" JUMPING UP"

We tend to ignore our dogs when they decide come to us, stand with us, and walk with us. However, when they jump on us we stop what we are doing, face them, speak to them, and put our hands on them until they are back on the ground. Then we immediately ignore them again! We feed them, open doors for them, and touch them, all while they jump. Obviously this is not helping the situation. We need to train the humans! It is important to avoid punishing (shouting "no", kneeing, etc) a dog who is jumping up because this could result in your dog no longer wanting to greet people or becoming fearful of them. When a dog does jump up on you it is best to turn your back on them and only give your attention to a dog with "4 on the floor".

Instead of teaching your dog "off" which requires him to be "up" in the first place, we can cue "sit" which most dogs have already been introduced to. In addition, we will attempt to teach him that jumping up does not lead to attention.

New doggie law: the only way to get attention from people is by keeping all four paws on the floor. The most important part of this training is to absolutely prevent him from being given attention for jumping up.

You will need at least 10 people to practice this lesson with your dog for him to understand that he will only get attention by remaining on the ground and that this rule applies for all humans. If you don't have enough people to help you practice, you can teach him to remain grounded for his family and then teach a really solid sit-stay to deal with others.

 It is also often helpful to desensitize your dog to the sound of the doorbell.

- ❖ **Teach him not to jump on family members:**
  It is easiest to teach your dog not to jump on the family and frequent visitors because he has many more opportunities for learning; also, everyone is (hopefully) on the same page and doesn't mind doing a little training. When you come in from outside and your dog begins to jump, say "oops" and immediately leave through the door. Repeat after a few seconds. Give him lots of attention when he is finally not jumping. Have everyone do the same exercise when coming home. If he is jumping on family other times besides when you enter, be sure to ignore that and put work into giving your dog attention when he is sitting.

- ❖ Teach him not to jump on everyone else:
  Prevention is key here, especially with a large dog. You can prevent a dog from jumping up by using a leash, tie-back, crate or gate. Until you have given your dog enough practice to know what you want him to do, you should make sure you are using one of these methods to prevent him from hurting anyone or by perhaps being rewarded by jumping and getting a nice pat.

GET YOUR DOG TO STOP BARKING.

Who hasn't walked past a house or an apartment doorway and heard the dog inside explode into barking? This specifically is for the people who live with those dogs the people shouting "dogalini, quiet!"

Why do dogs bark?

Dogs bark for many reasons, to solicit play, to signal that they're going on the offensive, to get our attention. They bark when they're stressed or bored or lonely. It's usually not hard to tell the difference. For instance, play barks are pitched higher than barks that convey a threat; a bored

and lonely dog may bark in a monotone for minutes or even hours at a stretch. Dogs suffering from separation anxiety can sound pretty desperate when they bark.

How To Get Your Dog To Stop Barking Inside

The kind of bark i'm talking about today bursts out loud and fast as the dog responds to something he hears or sees. Usually the dog rushes the door or window that the sight or sound is coming from. In brooklyn, where the row houses are set back from the sidewalk just a few feet, i sometimes see dogs pressing themselves flat against the windowpane as they bark at me. At some point, when the sight or noise that set them off has gone, the dog simmers down, maybe drops a few more sporadic barks, then goes back to whatever he was doing before. Of course, if provocative sights and sounds appear often, there may not be much of a break between bark fests.

And why is your dog doing this? Beats me! It could be a territorial behavior. Is it aggressive? Maybe. Whether we see it that way might depend on how intensely your dog barks and charges and how he responds to actual visitors. A dog may be frustrated because she can't greet the people or dogs she hears or sees. Herding dogs may be attempting to herd those moving bicycles and running kids. Some dogs make a lot of noise when startled.

Reward Your Dog When She Doesn't Bark At Things.

The beauty of all these tactics is that they don't depend on your being there to work. And, of course, a human being has to be present for training or behavior modification. When you're home with your dog, make it your business to notice times when he doesn't react to things, or when he reacts mildly and appropriately. For instance, he might get briefly alert and then lie down again. Either way, say "yes" quietly, or click to mark his good behavior, and give him a treat. When your dog's barking isn't always frenzied and out of control, it'll be easier for him to learn new behaviors. At that point you can begin teaching him a "now be quiet" cue.

When should you get professional help with your dog's barking?

And number 5 is this. If you've set your dog up to relax and snooze the day away by exercising him and cutting back the outdoor sound-and-light show, and you've conscientiously worked on rewarding quieter behavior and teaching him to stop barking on your cue, and you're still not getting anywhere, it's time to get competent in-person help. Your dog may be exceptionally anxious, or have a developing problem with aggression. A medical condition might be making him irritable. A smart professional will be alert to all these possibilities and can work with you herself or refer you appropriately. In short, the more your dog's behavior makes you wish for a quick fix, the better the odds that what's really called for is careful planning and professional help. Remember the tortoise and the hare!

HOW TO MAKE YOUR DOG COMFORTABLE IN THE WORLD AND IN THE VET'S OFFICE.

Find The Right Veterinarian

Does your dog hate the vet's office? It is common for dogs to have a fear of veterinarians. There is plenty of poking, prodding and other unpleasant things happening during your dog's typical vet visit, so it's no wonder he dislikes it. On the flip side, there are many dogs out there who absolutely love going to the vet. Have you ever wondered why? Here are some ways you can get your dog to love the veterinarian.

Do you have an amazing vet? Is your dog's vet clinic awesome? Choosing the right veterinarian can be a bit overwhelming, but you must take your dog's opinion into consideration. Do the staff members and veterinarian love interacting with your pet? Are they friendly and cheerful to pets and people? Most of all, do they truly want to get to know your dog and make him comfortable? If not, you might want to look for a new vet.

Get Your Dog Used To Being Handled.

Many dogs will not accept handling by a stranger, especially if they were not well-socialized as puppies. It's even worse if the type of handling is very unfamiliar. You can start doing small things at home to get your dog used to the feeling of a vet exam. First, familiarize yourself with the process of a basic vet examination. Then, conduct your own version of it at home. If your dog becomes used to being touched and handled in unusual ways, he might be more accepting of it from a stranger. He will likely do even better if you carefully and gradually introduce him to the strangers (the vet and staff).

Don't Force It

The most important rule when working to get any dog or puppy comfortable being handled is never to force anything. This is not an exercise in controlling your dog, but rather training a dog to be relaxed and comfortable. So if you want to train a dog to be comfortable with having his nails trimmed, don't start off by holding him down and forcing him to accept the grooming.

Visit The Vet Clinic Just For Fun

Ideally, you will get your dog used to the vet before he actually has a health problem. Done right, your dog may actually get really excited about the vet's office. Plan visits to the vet just to socialize and take a look around. I call these "happy social visits." Pick a time when your dog is feeling well and does not need to see the vet. Ask your vet clinic when their not-so-busy times are. You should not need an appointment.

Take your dog for a car ride or walk to the clinic. Get excited about it and reward your dog for getting a little excited or simply being calm and relaxed. If your dog's reaction is positive, go inside the clinic, meeting and greeting the staff up front. Everyone should be happy and calm, making sure not to overwhelm your dog. Treats should be given if your dog can tolerate them. If you notice your dog is getting nervous, it's time to leave. The first few times you do this, it might be as simple as breezing through the lobby for 10 seconds. Eventually, you may notice the wagging tail as you approach the door. When ready, try scheduling a simple appointment for something like a basic exam.